She Laid Him in a Manger

Woodcuts from the Missal
published by L. de Giunta in Venice, 1504
from the Rare Books Room
of Saint Meinrad Archabbey Library

Text Translation by Harry Hagan, O.S.B.
©2010 Saint Meinrad Archabbey
Printed in the United States of America
Abbey Press Publications
St. Meinrad, IN 47577

She Laid Him in a Manger

The Birth of Jesus from the Gospels of Matthew and Luke

Harry Hagan, O.S.B.

ABBEY PRESS

St. Meinrad, IN 47577

To all those who tell this story
over and over in their own words
to new generations.

Introduction

For Christians, the story of Christ's birth tells of God's coming among us as one like ourselves, and we tell this story again and again in many ways in order to lay hold of its power.

This little book offers to the reader the whole Christmas story as told by Matthew and Luke. While the account in each gospel has its own integrity, we typically read them together to grasp and explore the mystery of Christ's incarnation and epiphany to the world.

This translation has been taken from the Greek with an eye to both the Latin Vulgate of Saint Jerome and the King James Version that shaped biblical language in English. The translation seeks to be simple and direct so that the reader can feel the claim of this story today.

The woodcuts come from a volume in the Rare Books Room of the Saint Meinrad Archabbey Library, a Missal published in 1504 by Luc Antonio Giunta at Venice, just 50 years after publication of the Gutenberg Bible.

These pictures tell the story in their own way and remind us that we belong to a great tradition celebrating this mystery of Christ.

Harry Hagan, O.S.B.
March 25, 2010
Feast of the Annunciation

The Annunciation to Mary

Luke 1:26-38

In the sixth month, the angel Gabriel was sent by God to a city of Galilee named Nazareth, to a virgin engaged to a man named Joseph of the house of David, and the virgin's name was Mary.

And coming to her, the angel said:
  "Hail, full of grace! The Lord is with you."

Now she was troubled by the word and wondered what kind of greeting this could be.

And the angel said to her:
  "Do not be afraid, Mary,
  for you have found grace with God.
  Behold, you shall conceive in your womb

and bring forth a Son,
and you shall name him Jesus.
He shall be great,
and he shall be called
the Son of the Most High.
The Lord God shall give to him
the throne of his father David,
and he shall be king
over the house of Jacob forever.
And of his Kingdom there shall be no end."

Then Mary said to the angel,
"How shall this be
since I do not know a man in this way?"

The angel answered and said to her,
"The Holy Spirit shall come upon you,
and the power of the Most High
shall overshadow you.
Therefore, the one to be born
shall be called holy
the Son of God.
And behold, Elizabeth, your cousin!
She also has conceived a son in her old age,

and this is the sixth month for her
who was called barren.
For with God no word shall be impossible."

And Mary said,

"Behold, I am the servant of the Lord.
Let it be done to me according to your word."

And the angel departed from her.

Joseph's Dream

Matthew 1:18-25

Now the birth of Jesus Christ happened in this way.
His mother Mary was engaged to Joseph, but before they came
together, she was found to have a child in her womb from the
Holy Spirit.

Joseph, her husband, being a just man and not wanting to disgrace her, wanted to divorce her secretly.

While he thought about these things, behold, the angel of the
Lord appeared to him in a dream and said:
"Joseph, son of David,
do not be afraid to take Mary for your wife
because the one she has conceived
is from the Holy Spirit.
And she will give birth to a son.
You shall name him Jesus,
for he will save his people from their sins."

Now this was all done
so that what the Lord had spoken by the prophet
could be fulfilled—saying:
> *"Behold, a virgin shall be with child,*
> *and shall give birth to a son,*
> *and they shall name him Emmanuel,*
> *which is translated, 'God is with us.'"*

When Joseph arose from sleep, he did as the angel of the Lord
had commanded him and took her for his wife. He did not
know her until she gave birth to a son, and he called his name
Jesus.

The Decree of Caesar Augustus

Luke 2:1-5

And it came to pass in those days, that a decree went out from Caesar Augustus that there should be a census of the whole world. This was the first census, and it took place while Quirinius was governor of Syria, and they all went to their home towns to be registered.

So Joseph went up from the city of Nazareth in Galilee to Judah, to the city of David called Bethlehem because he was of the house and family of David. He went up to be registered with Mary, to whom he was engaged, and she was with child.

The Birth of Jesus

Luke 2:6-7

While they were there, the days for her to give birth to the child were completed, and she gave birth to a firstborn son and wrapped him in swaddling clothes, and laid him in a manger.

She laid him in a manger because there was no room for them in the inn.

The Shepherds and the Angel Host

Luke 2:8-12

In the same region there were shepherds living out in the fields and watching their flocks by night.

And behold, an angel of the Lord stood above them, and the glory of the Lord shone round about them, and they were much afraid. And the angel said to them:

"Do not be afraid,
for behold, I bring you a gospel of great joy
which is for all the people.
For to you is born this day
in the city of David
a Savior who is Christ the Lord.
And this shall be a sign for you:
you shall find the babe
wrapped in swaddling clothes,
lying in a manger."

Glory to God in the Highest

Luke 2:13-15

And suddenly there was with the angel a multitude of the heavenly host praising God and saying:

"*Glory to God in the highest,*
and on earth peace to people of good will."

When the angels had left them for heaven, the shepherds said to one another,

"Let us go now to Bethlehem
and see what has happened
this word
that the Lord has made known to us."

The Shepherds
at the Manger

Luke 2:16-21

And they went with haste and found Mary and Joseph and the babe lying in a manger.

After seeing this, they made known the word spoken to them about this child.

And all those who heard wondered at those things spoken to them by the shepherds.

Now Mary treasured all these words and pondered them in her heart.

The shepherds went back glorifying and praising God for all the things that they had heard and seen—just as it had been spoken to them.

And when eight days were fulfilled, they circumcised the child, and he was called Jesus,
the name that the angel had called him before he was conceived in the womb.

Herod and the Wise Men

Matthew 2:1-8

Now Jesus was born in Bethlehem of Judah in the days of Herod the king.

Behold, wise men from the east came
to Jerusalem and said:
  "Where is he who is born
  King of the Jews?
  For we have seen his star in the east,
  and we have come to worship him."

When Herod the king heard these things, he was troubled and all Jerusalem with him.

He gathered all the chief priests and scribes of the people together and asked where the Christ was to be born.

And they said to him:
    "In Bethlehem of Judah,
for this was written down by the prophet,

> *And you Bethlehem in the land of Judah*
>   *you are by no means least*
>   *of the princes of Judah,*
> *for out of you shall come a ruler*
>   *who shall rule over my people Israel."*

Then Herod called the wise men secretly and found out from them the time when the star had appeared. He sent them to Bethlehem and said,
    "Go and search carefully for the young child.
    Then, when you have found him,
    bring a report back to me
    so that I too may go and worship him."

C In epiphanía domíni. Statio ad
sanctum petrum.   Introitus.

Ece aduenit
dñator dñis:τ
regnuz in ma
nu eius τ pote
stas τ iperiũ.
ps. Deus iu
diciũ tuum re
gi da τ iustiti
az tuã filio re
gis. ℣. Glia.

Oeus qui ho Oro
dierna die vnigenitũ tuũ gétí
bus stella duce reuelasti:ⱷcede ppi
tius:vt qui iaz te er fide cognouim⁹
vſⱷ ad ⱷtemplandã ſpeciem tue cel
ſitudinis perducamur. Per eundé.

S Lectio eſaie pꝛophete. ir.caꝑ.
Urge illuminare hierłz qꝛ ue
nit lumé tuũ τ glía dñi ſuper te oꝛta
eſt.qꝛ ecce tenebꝛe operient terrã : τ
caligo pplos.Sup te aũt oꝛieꞇ dñs:τ
gloꝛia eius in te videbiꞇ.Et ambula
bunt gentes in lumine tuo:τ reges
in ſplendoꝛe oꝛtus tui.Leua i circui
tu oculos tuos τ vide.oés iſti ꝗgre
gati ſunt venerunt tibi. Filij tui de

The Star Returns

Matthew 2:9-10

After listening to the king, they went on, and behold, the star that they had seen in the east went before them until it came to rest over the place where the child was.

When they saw the star, they rejoiced with an exceedingly great joy.

The Wise Men Offer Their Gifts

Matthew 2:11-12

They came into the house and saw the young child with Mary his mother.

They fell down and worshiped him.

Opening their treasures, they presented him
        with gifts of gold
        and frankincense
        and myrrh.

Warned in a dream not to return to Herod, they returned to their own country by another way.

The Flight into Egypt

Matthew 2:13-15

After they had departed,
behold, the angel of the Lord appeared
to Joseph in a dream and said,

> "Arise, and take the young child and his mother,
> and flee to Egypt.
> Stay there until I tell you,
> for Herod is going to search for the young child
> in order to kill him."

Getting up that night,
Joseph took the young child and his mother
and set out for Egypt.
They stayed there until the death of Herod
to fulfill what the Lord said by the prophet:
> *"Out of Egypt I have called my son."*

The Slaying of the Holy Innocents

Matthew 2:16-18

When Herod saw
that he had been tricked by the wise men,
he was very angry.
He sent people to kill
all the children in and around Bethlehem
that were two years old and under
because this fit with the time
that he had carefully ascertained
from the wise men.

This fulfilled what the prophet Jeremiah said:
> *"A voice was heard in Ramah*
> *weeping and much mourning.*
> *Rachel was weeping for her children*
> *and would not be comforted*
> *because they were no more."*

The Return from Egypt

Matthew 2:19-23

When Herod was dead,
behold an angel of the Lord appeared
in a dream to Joseph in Egypt and said:
>"Arise and take the young child and his mother,
>and go to the land of Israel,
>>for those who sought the life of the young child
>>are now dead."

So Joseph arose
and took the child and his mother
and came into the land of Israel.

When Joseph heard
that Archelaus was king in Judah

in place of his father Herod,
he was afraid to go there.
Being warned in a dream,
he went on to the region of Galilee
and came to dwell in a city called Nazareth.
This fulfilled what the prophets had said:

"He shall be called a Nazarene."

*"I am with you always,
until the end of the age."*

Matthew 28:20

We Have a Story to Tell

Harry Hagan, O.S.B.

The story of the birth of Christ is well known, perhaps one of the best-known stories in the world. Many people first heard this story from their parents at home while putting up the Christmas crib, and so the retelling of this story unlocks many levels of mystery.

The story comes to us from two gospels: Matthew and Luke. Each gospel has its own unique perspective and emphasis, and they come together in our own minds to create our own understanding of the story.

Matthew's Gospel focuses on Joseph who was "just." This word "just" identifies him as one who was faithful to the Torah, the teaching of Moses. Having discovered that his betrothed was with child by another, he decides to do what a "just man" should do and divorce her. However, he was also a caring man who did not want to disgrace her, and so he planned to do it secretly. In a very few words, Matthew provides us with a large understanding of this "just" man.

An angel appears to Joseph in a dream and tells him an amazing story about a virgin conceiving of the Holy Spirit. The angel also tells Joseph that he is to name the child "Jesus," who "will save his people from their sins." All of this will happen to fulfill Isaiah's prophecy of a virgin with a child named Emmanuel—"God with us." Joseph believes this unbelievable dream and becomes "just" according to the Kingdom of God that is coming near. The word "just" and "justice"—also translated "righteous" and "righteousness"—plays a key role in Matthew's Gospel, but it is the new justice of the Kingdom. Therefore, Matthew 6:33 says: "Seek first the Kingdom of God and its justice, and all the rest will be given to you as well." The justice of Joseph allows him to go beyond what he expected and to become part of the fulfillment of Isaiah's prophecy.

Matthew also gives us the story of the three wise men seeking the newborn king. Their coming from the East foretells a kingdom without borders, a kingdom for all nations. Quickly, however, the newborn king threatens earthly kingship and its dependence on violence. The death of the children of Bethlehem portends the crucifixion. Again, a dream alerts Joseph, who is able to protect this child named Jesus by fleeing to Egypt. Still, the cross casts its shadow over the story.

Luke's Gospel focuses more on Mary. It tells us the story of the angel Gabriel's word to this unsuspecting virgin and of her acceptance: "Let it be done to me according to your word." In due course the days are completed, and she gives birth, and she wraps the child, and she lays him in the manger. Luke's Gospel gives prominence to women in general, but none receive more honor than the mother of the Savior who will treasure all these things in her heart.

Luke's Gospel also pays special attention to those at the margins of society for whom the Gospel holds great promise. The first to make their appearance from the edge of society are the shepherds, who were regarded with caution by the settled people of the towns. Still, the shepherd was an ancient image for the king. So these unimportant people, living in the fields at the edge, find themselves confronted by an angel with startling news and then by a multitude of heavenly host singing "Glory!" The Gospel tells us that they, after seeing for themselves, made known the word spoken to them, and so they become the first to tell the Gospel.

The stories from these two Gospels come together for each of us to form one story. This little book offers its reader a chance to confront once again the stories as they are given to us in the Scriptures. As always, the Scriptures challenge us to make these stories our own, so that we, too, can make known what has been spoken to us.

Fr. Harry Hagan, O.S.B., is a monk and priest of Saint
Meinrad Archabbey in Indiana. He did his doctoral studies
in Scripture at the Pontifical Biblical Institute in Rome and
teaches Scripture at Saint Meinrad Seminary and School of
Theology. He has translated several monastic works and a
number of Latin hymns for the Liturgy of the Hours.